THIS BOOK BELONGS TO

WHO LOVES
TO GET OUT

ANSWERS CAN BE FOUND AT THE BACK OF THE BOOK

WITH THANKS TO

David Burnie – Natural-history consultant

Sunita Gahir – Production adviser

A NOTE FROM THE BUTTERFLY

Please don't collect or eat any of the things
that you find outside – you may harm the
animals, the plants or yourself.

First published in Great Britian as *Get Out: Nature Puzzles & Games* in 2013
This revised edition published in 2016 by Fine Feather Press Limited
The Coach House, Elstead Road, Farnham, Surrey GU10 1JE

2 4 6 8 10 9 7 5 3 1

A CIP catalogue record is available from the British Library

ISBN: 978-1-908489-29-6

Printed in Shenzhen, China by C&C Offset Printing Co

MIX
Paper from
responsible sources
FSC® C008047

FSC
www.fsc.org

www.finefeatherpress.com

GET OUT!

NATURE ACTIVITY BOOK

The world is mud–luscious...
and puddle wonderful...

CAZ BUCKINGHAM &
ANDREA PINNINGTON

FFP
Fine Feather Press

GET OUT AND LISTEN TO SPRING

buzzzzz!

bee

Have a good look at these spring things, then turn the page.

munch!

caterpillar

tseep! tseep!

rabbit

sniff! sniff!

dunnock

tik-ik-ik-ik!

bud

eggshells

robin

catkins

crack!

snowdrops

baaa! baaa!

lamb

WHAT CAN YOU REMEMBER?

Write or draw any of the spring things you can remember from the previous page.

HELP THE WORKER BEE

Can you find the way through the
honeycomb maze?

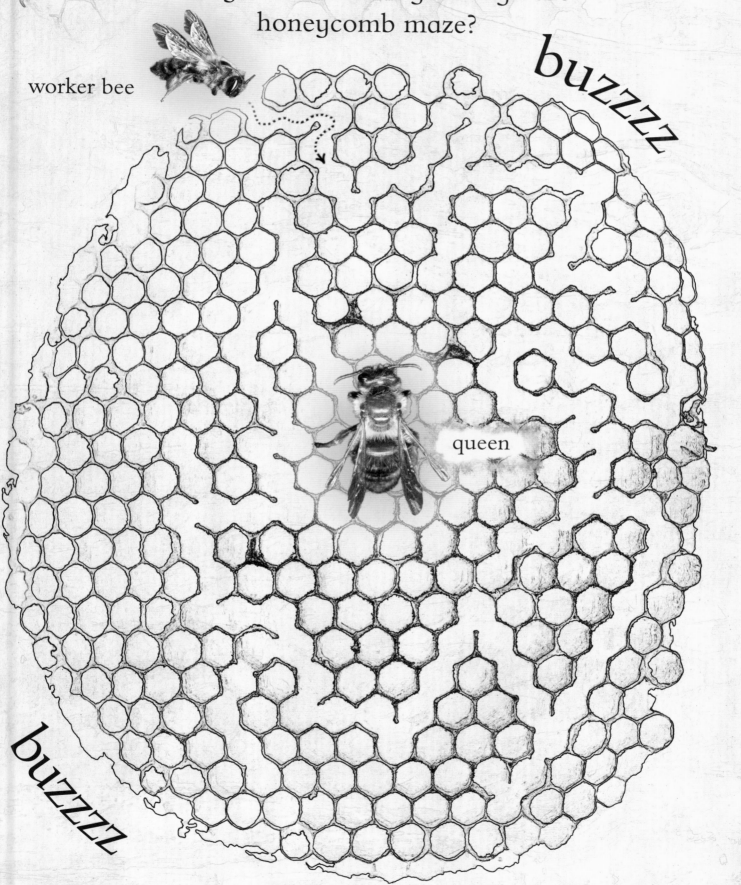

worker bee

buzzzz

queen

buzzzz

CAN YOU GUESS?

Here are some close-up pictures of things you would find outside. Write down what you think they are in the boxes below.

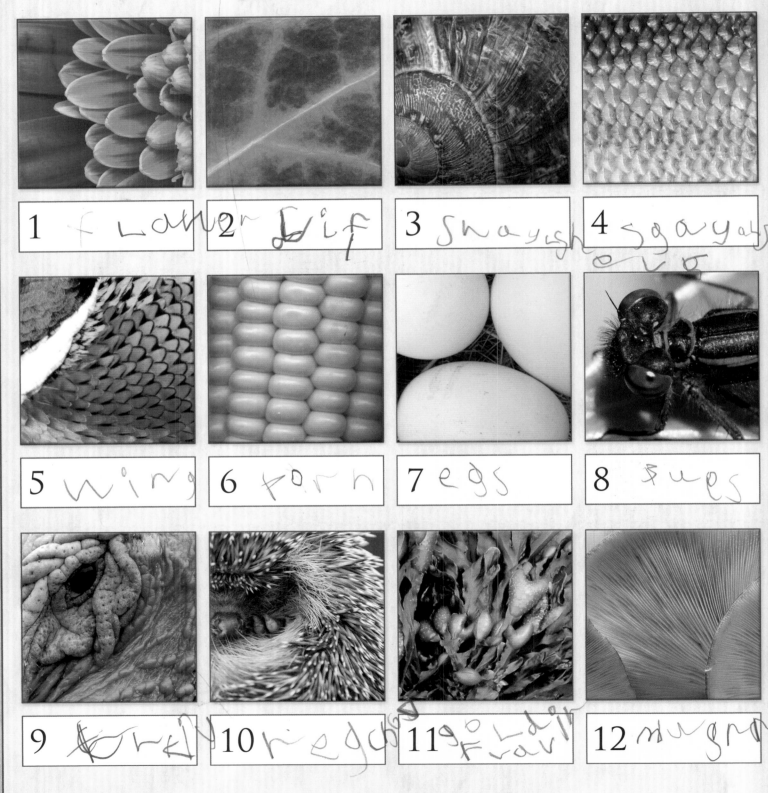

1 flawer
2 lif
3 snaygsh
4 sgayays

5 wing
6 forn
7 egs
8 sues

9 trely
10 riegdog
11 oldir frarlr
12 mugra

WHAT DO I TURN INTO?

Draw a line connecting each young
animal to its adult form.

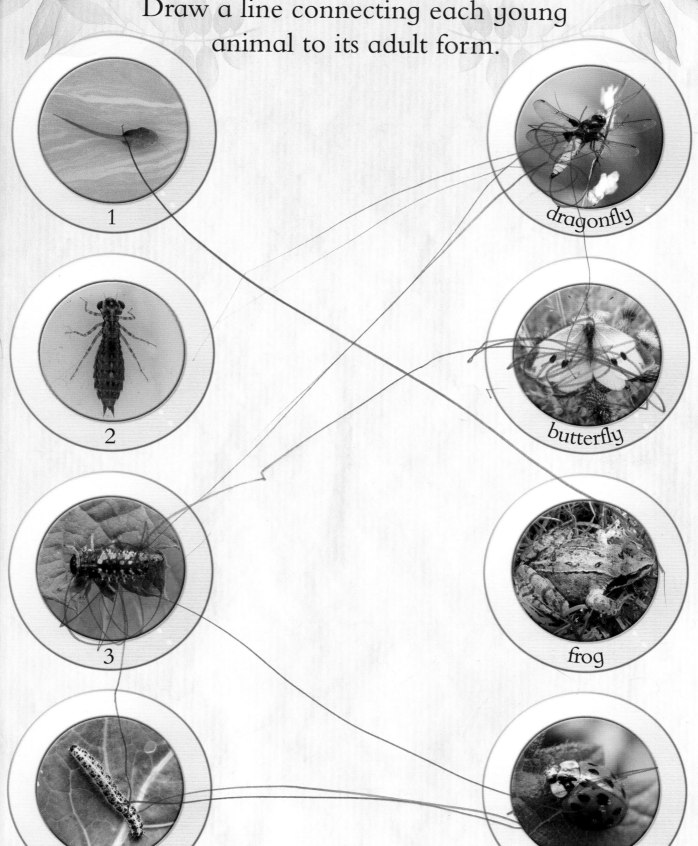

1

2

3

4

dragonfly

butterfly

frog

ladybird

FIND THE FAMILIES

There are six different animal families here.

fawn

drake

ewe

bull

chick

cow

stag

billy

lamb

Give each animal family the same colour frames.

hen

ram

kid

doe

duckling

cockerel

calf

nanny

duck

pig

stag beetle

COLOUR THE ANIMALS
AND GUESS

great tit

lizard

Invertebrates
Cold-blooded animals
with no backbone,
such as spiders, snails,
insects and worms.

Fish
Scaly creatures
that live underwater,
breathe with gills and
have backbones.

Amphibians
Amphibians spend
time in water and on
land. They lay eggs
and are cold-blooded.

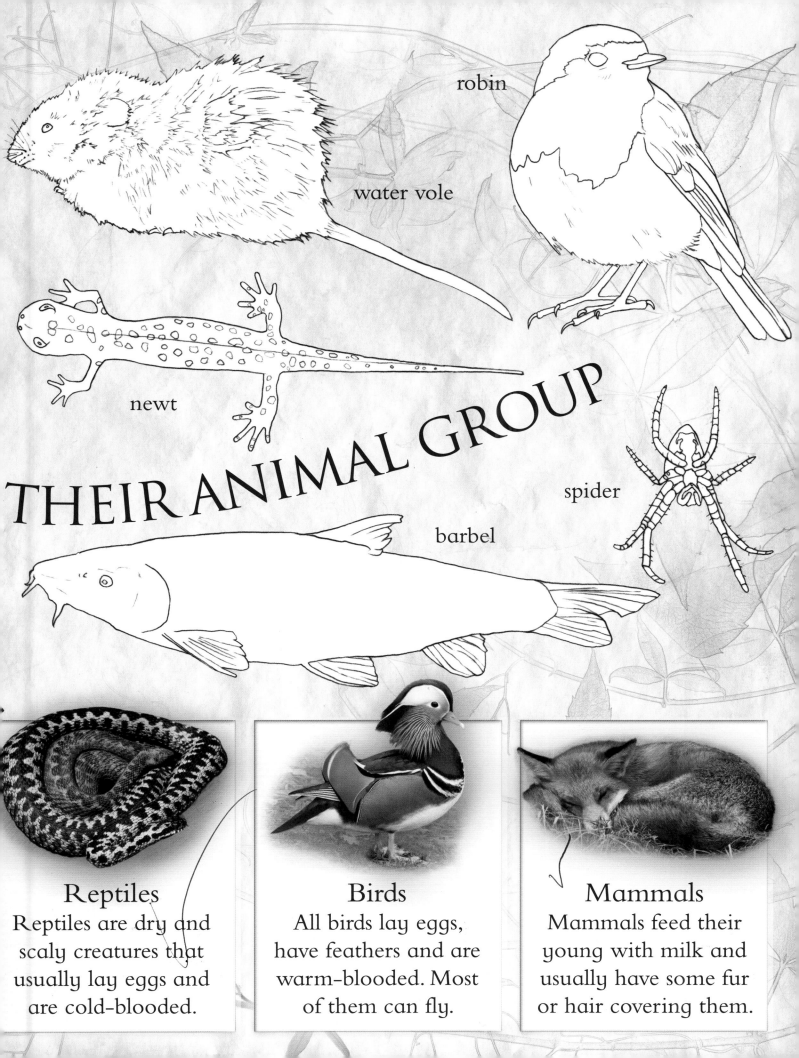

robin

water vole

newt

spider

THEIR ANIMAL GROUP

barbel

Reptiles
Reptiles are dry and scaly creatures that usually lay eggs and are cold-blooded.

Birds
All birds lay eggs, have feathers and are warm-blooded. Most of them can fly.

Mammals
Mammals feed their young with milk and usually have some fur or hair covering them.

TICK THE TRUE FACTS

1

There are more beetles than any other type of animal.

2

Owls hoot at night to let cars know they are coming.

3

Fat hen, common mouse-ear and sneezewort are all names of wildflowers.

4

Young swifts can fly for three years without stopping.

5

If a lizard loses its tail, it grows back a new one.

6

Johnny was the name of the first talking sheep.

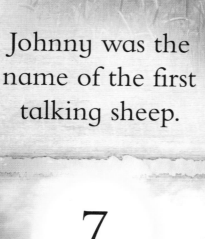

☐

7

It's always sunny in England.

☐

8

Rabbits use dewdrops to clean their fur.

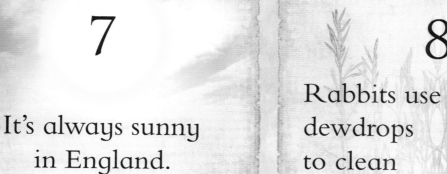

☑

9

A collection of trees is called a barking.

☑

10

Cuckoos lay eggs in other birds' nests.

☑

butterfly

GET OUT
AND
FEEL THE
SUMMER

dandelion

Have a good look at these summer
things, then turn the page.

smooth

beetle

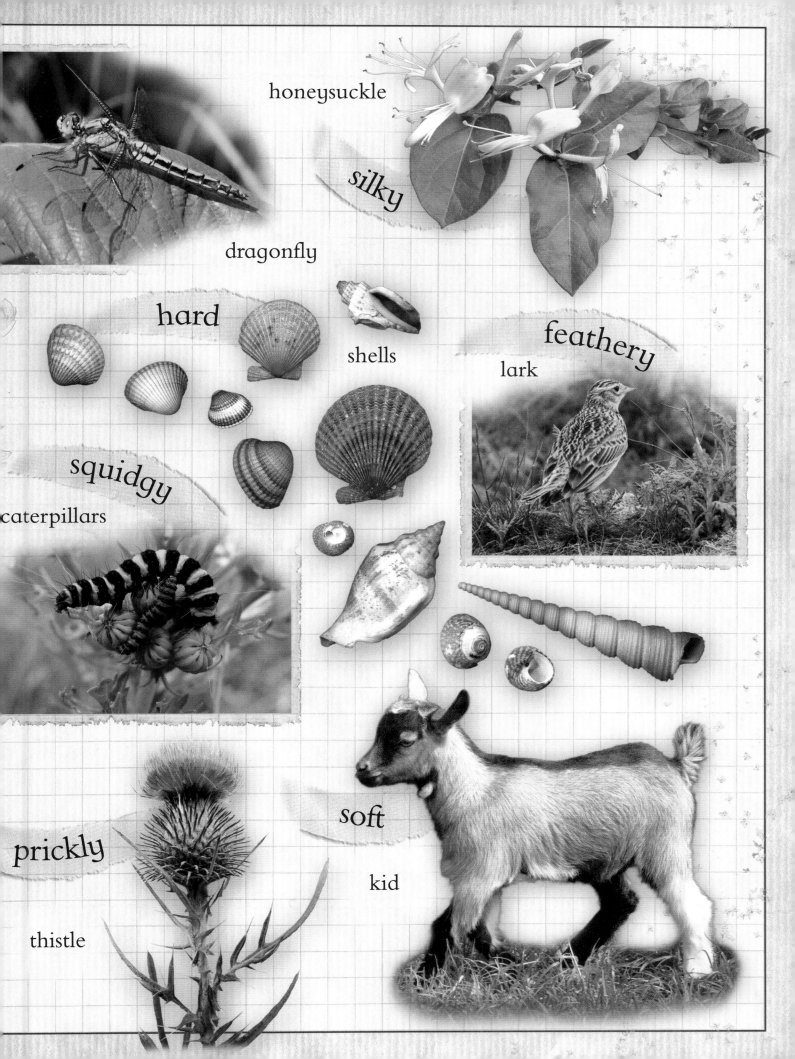

honeysuckle

silky

dragonfly

hard

shells

feathery

lark

squidgy

caterpillars

soft

prickly

kid

thistle

WHAT CAN YOU REMEMBER?

Write or draw any of the summer things you can
remember from the previous page.

WHO'S HIDING HERE?

How many bugs can you find hiding in this picture?

WHO'S MY PARTNER?

Match the male birds opposite to the females below, writing their names in underneath.

chaffinch

peahen

hen

mallard

pheasant

sparrow

1 _____ 4 _____

2 _____ 5 _____

3 _____ 6 _____

LOOK CLOSELY

Learn how to tell a dragonfly from a damselfly and a butterfly from a moth, then colour them in.

DAMSELFLY

eyes at the side

thinner body

wings together when resting

DRAGONFLY

eyes together

wings held out at rest

thicker body

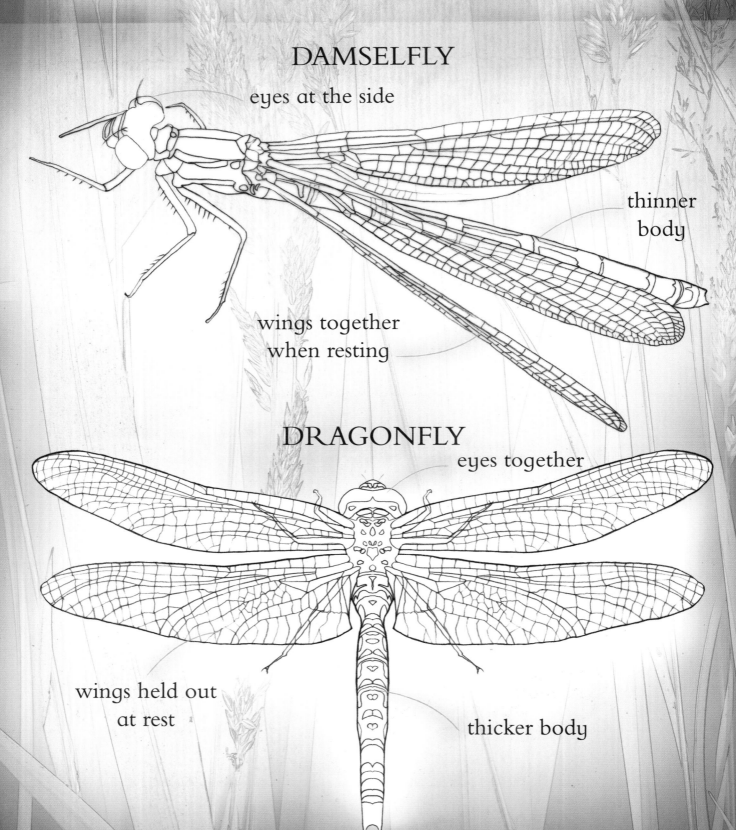

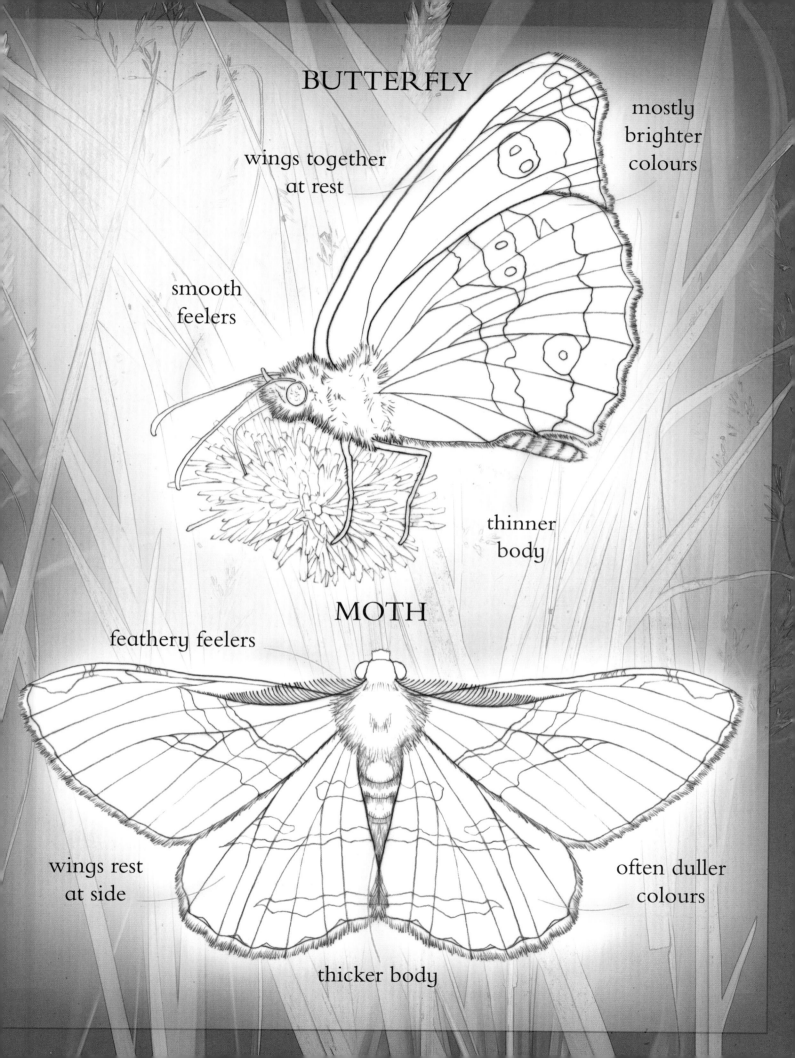

BUTTERFLY

wings together
at rest

mostly
brighter
colours

smooth
feelers

thinner
body

MOTH

feathery feelers

wings rest
at side

often duller
colours

thicker body

FIND THE MATCHING PAIRS

There are 15 pairs of shells.
Can you find them all?

Write in the numbers of the matching shells.

CAN YOU GUESS?

Here are some close-up pictures of things you would find outside. Write down what you think they are in the boxes below.

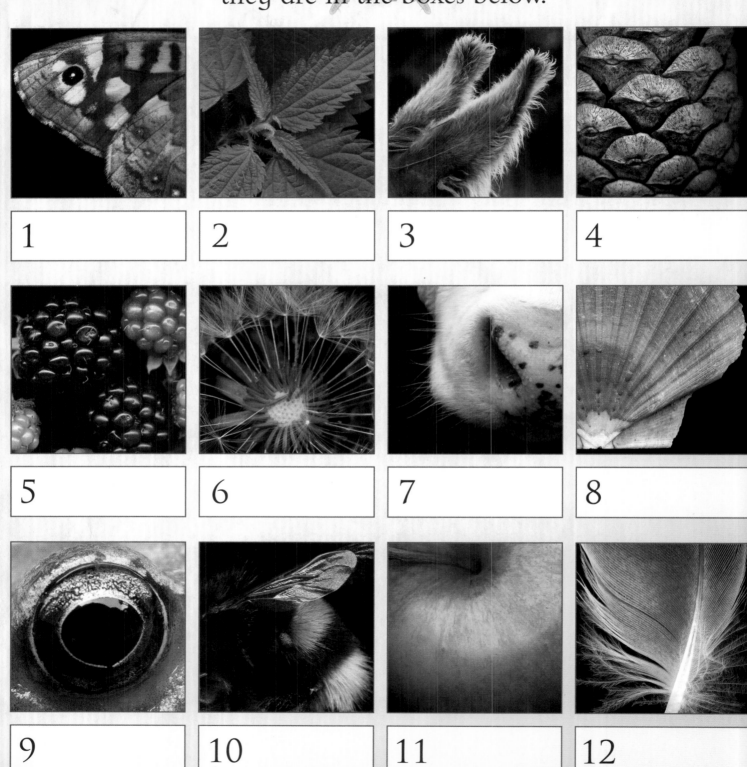

1

2

3

4

5

6

7

8

9

10

11

12

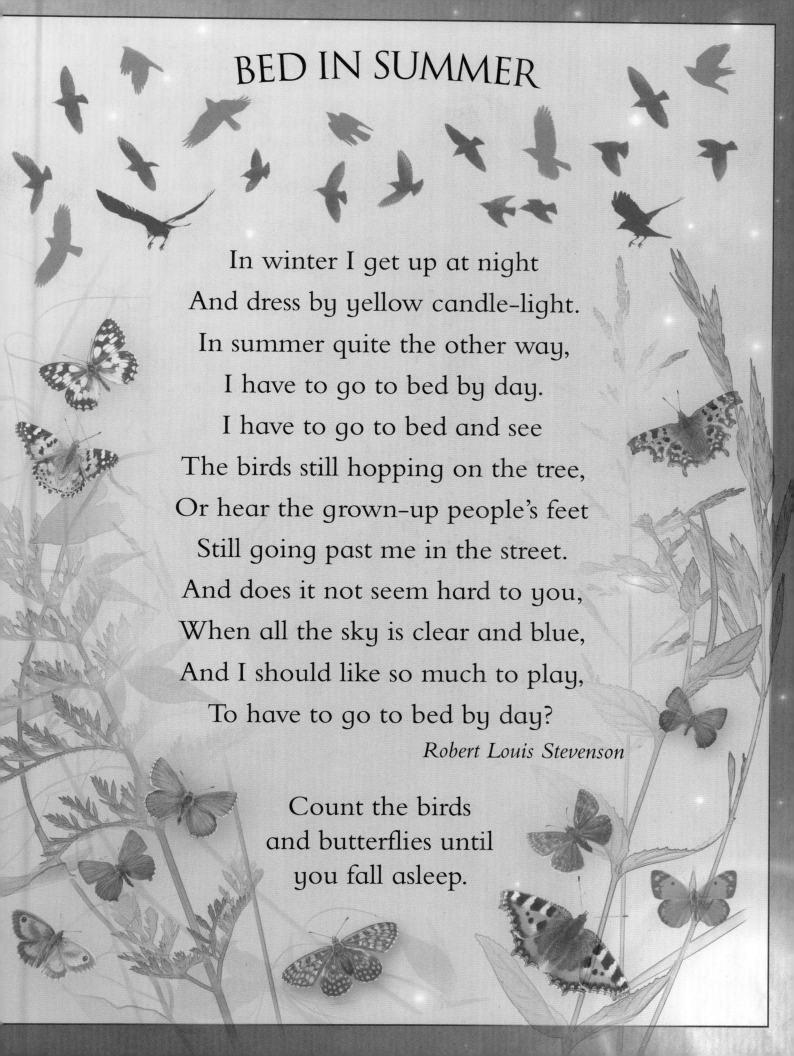

BED IN SUMMER

In winter I get up at night
And dress by yellow candle-light.
In summer quite the other way,
I have to go to bed by day.

I have to go to bed and see
The birds still hopping on the tree,
Or hear the grown-up people's feet
Still going past me in the street.

And does it not seem hard to you,
When all the sky is clear and blue,
And I should like so much to play,
To have to go to bed by day?

Robert Louis Stevenson

Count the birds
and butterflies until
you fall asleep.

SPOT THE DIFFERENCE

Can you spot 10 differences between the pictures?

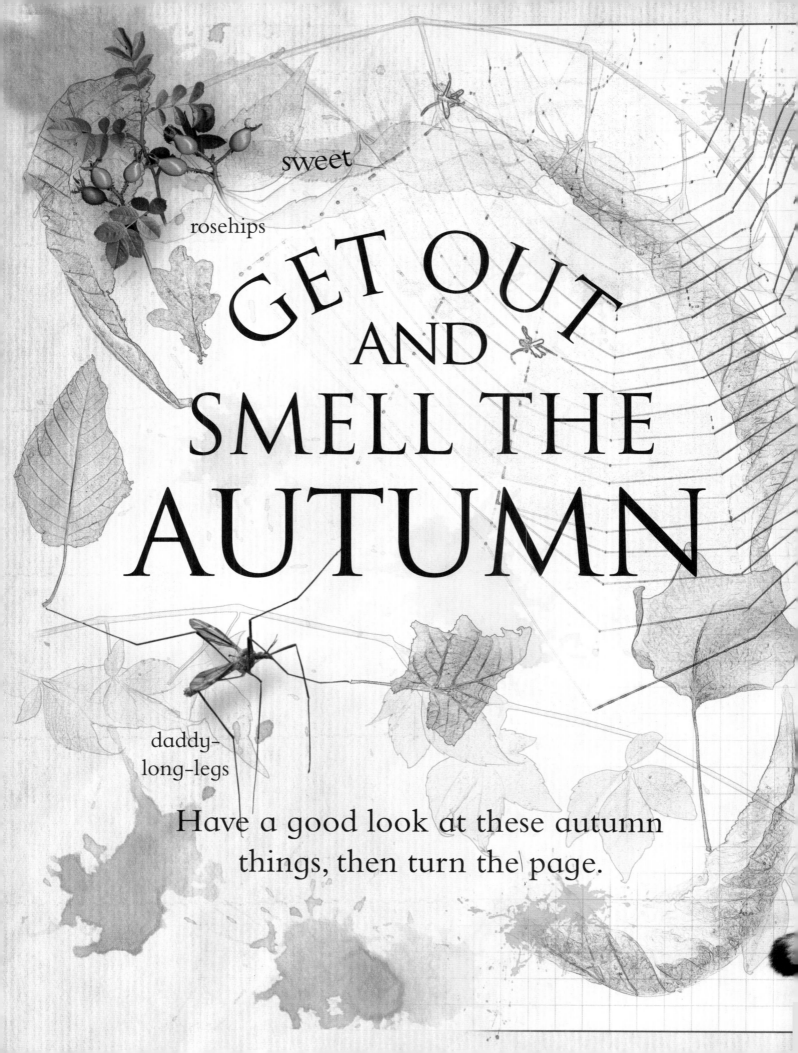

sweet

rosehips

GET OUT
AND
SMELL THE
AUTUMN

daddy-
long-legs

Have a good look at these autumn
things, then turn the page.

red squirrel

earthy

toadstools

conkers

smoky   bonfire

fruity

blackberries

musty

fox

autumn leaves

WHAT CAN YOU REMEMBER?

Write or draw any of the autumn things you can remember from the previous page.

DRAW THE OTHER HALF

Complete the other halves of the autumn leaves
and then colour them in.

maple   oak   horse chestnut

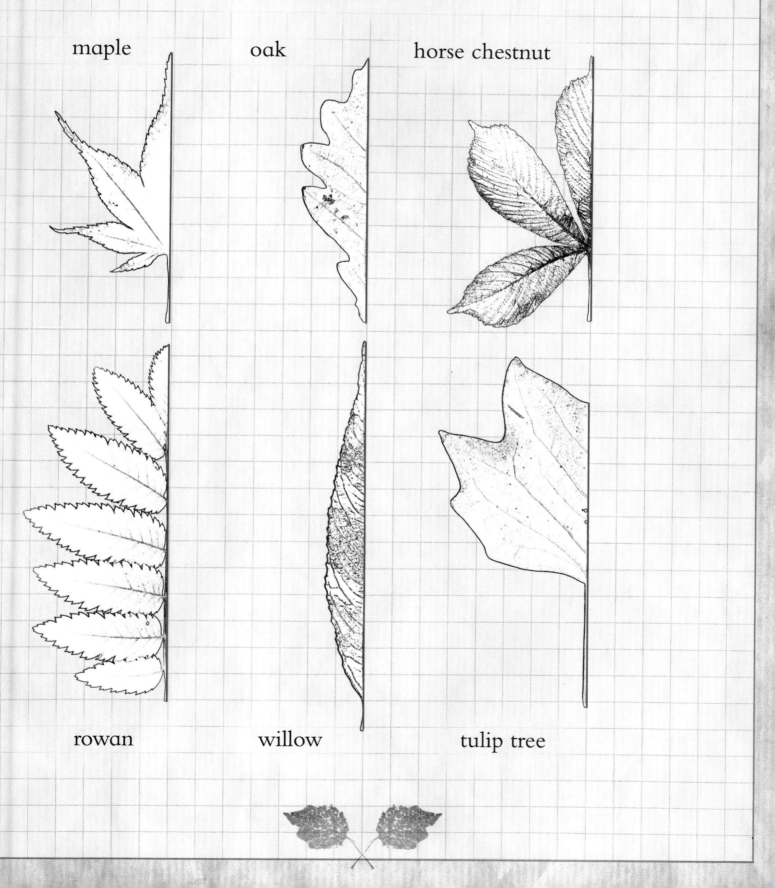

rowan   willow   tulip tree

MISSING CREATURES

Draw some spiders and flies onto the spider's web.

COLOUR AND COMPLETE

Guess what these birds eat by looking at their beaks.

jackdaw

Sharp beak for eating most foods.

parakeet

Hooked beak for cracking nuts.

robin

Small beak for feeding on worms and insects.

blackbird

Sharp, pointy beak for pulling up worms.

duck

Wide, flat beak for sifting food in water.

goose

Bright red beak – good for scaring children!

Copy the beaks from the page
opposite, and then colour in the birds.

NAME THAT GROUP

Tick the correct answers.

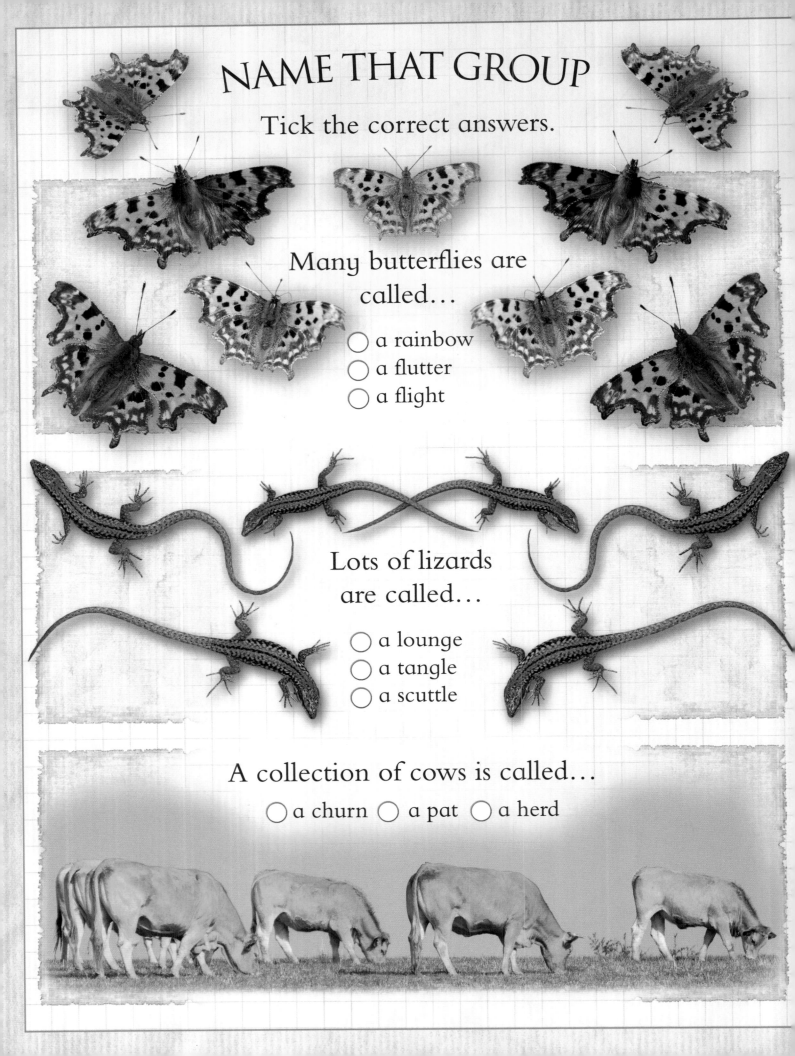

Many butterflies are called…

○ a rainbow
○ a flutter
○ a flight

Lots of lizards are called…

○ a lounge
○ a tangle
○ a scuttle

A collection of cows is called…

○ a churn   ○ a pat   ○ a herd

An alarming number
of geese is called…

○ a gaggle
○ a giggle
○ a scream

Many turkeys are called…
○ a pain ○ a gang ○ a gobble

Lots of otters are called… ○ a raft ○ a worry ○ a party

SPOT THE DIFFERENCE

Find 10 differences between the pictures.

FIND THE LETTERS

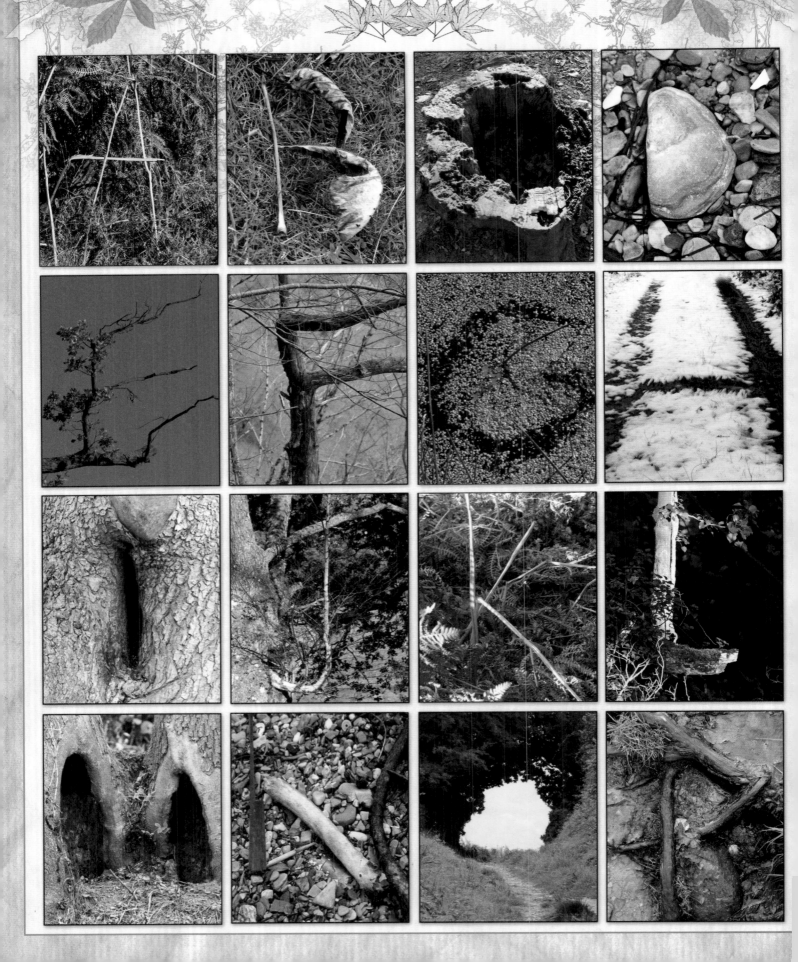

Can you spot every letter of the alphabet when
you go outside? Here are some examples.

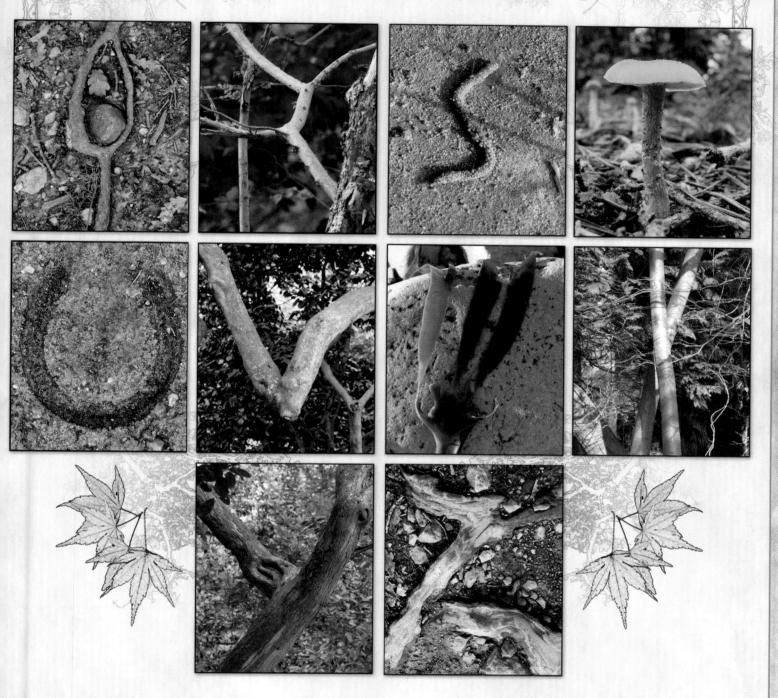

Tick off the letters below as you find them.

ABCDEFGHIJKLMN
OPQRSTUVWXYZ

mistletoe

snowflakes

GET OUT
AND
SEE THE
WINTER

Have a good look at these winter
things, then turn the page.

lichen

green

grey

heron

red

yew

black

tree

dog tracks

white

swan

brown

larch

WHAT CAN YOU REMEMBER?

Write or draw any of the winter things you can remember from the previous page.

ODD ONE OUT

Circle the things that you would not see in winter.

bumblebee

snowdrop

thrush

icicle

butterfly

harebell

holly

dead leaf

duckling

frost

TICK THE TRUE FACTS

1 Holly is the main ingredient in Christmas pudding. ☐

2 Snowy owls prefer hot weather. ☐

3 Mistle thrushes sing when storms are approaching. ☐

4 If you see a white dog in November, snow will soon fall. ☐

5 Monarch butterflies travel 2,500 miles to Mexico each winter. ☐

6

Hibernation is when animals sleep during the cold weather.

7

Chionophobia is the fear of snow.

8

Pheasants move twice as fast in the cold.

9

Swallows fly to the Arctic in September.

10

A stoat's fur turns white in the winter.

WHAT CAN YOU FIND?

There's always something interesting to find outside.
Here are some things to look out for on a winter walk.

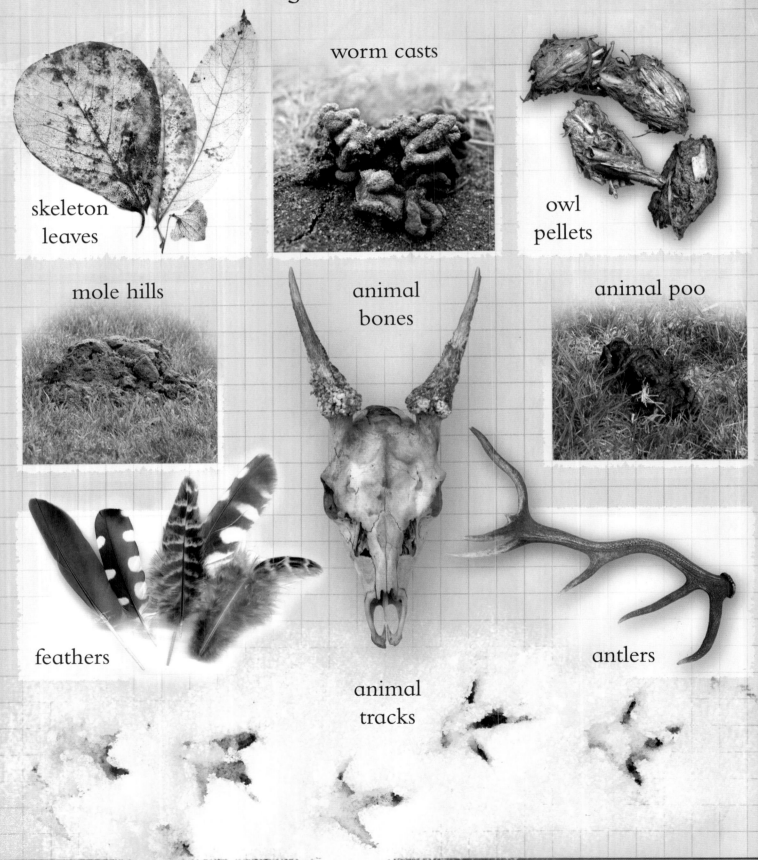

skeleton
leaves

worm casts

owl
pellets

mole hills

animal
bones

animal poo

feathers

antlers

animal
tracks

Draw or write below the name of any nature things you find outside.

SOLVE THE RIDDLES

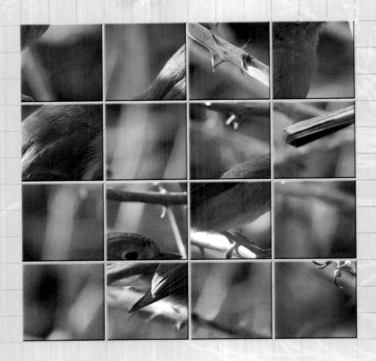

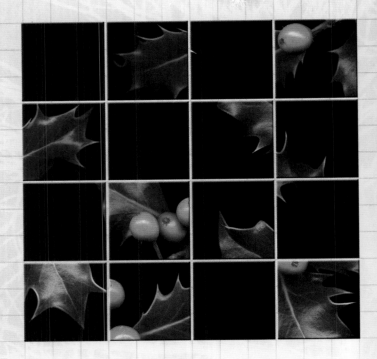

I live in gardens, woods and parks
– I'm not a blue tit, jay or lark.
I have two wings, one tail, one beak,
I love to sing but cannot speak.

WHAT AM I?

My leaves have nasty pointy edges.
I stand alone or grow in hedges.
My berries may look red and sweet
but they are POISONOUS to eat.

WHAT AM I?

Draw or write your answers in the boxes.

You may not see us trotting by
for we are really rather shy.
We move around without a sound.
Look out for tracks upon the ground.

WHAT ARE WE?

We form long spikes when it is cold
and winter starts to take its hold.
But if it is a sunny day
my friends and I just melt away.

WHAT ARE WE?

COLOUR THE CRYSTALS

When it is really cold, tiny ice crystals like these stick together and fall through the sky as snowflakes.

COMPLETE THE PICTURES

Can you join the dots, trace the outlines
and finish the wintry patterns below?

FILL IN THE SEASONAL CIRCLES

February

March

January

December

November

October

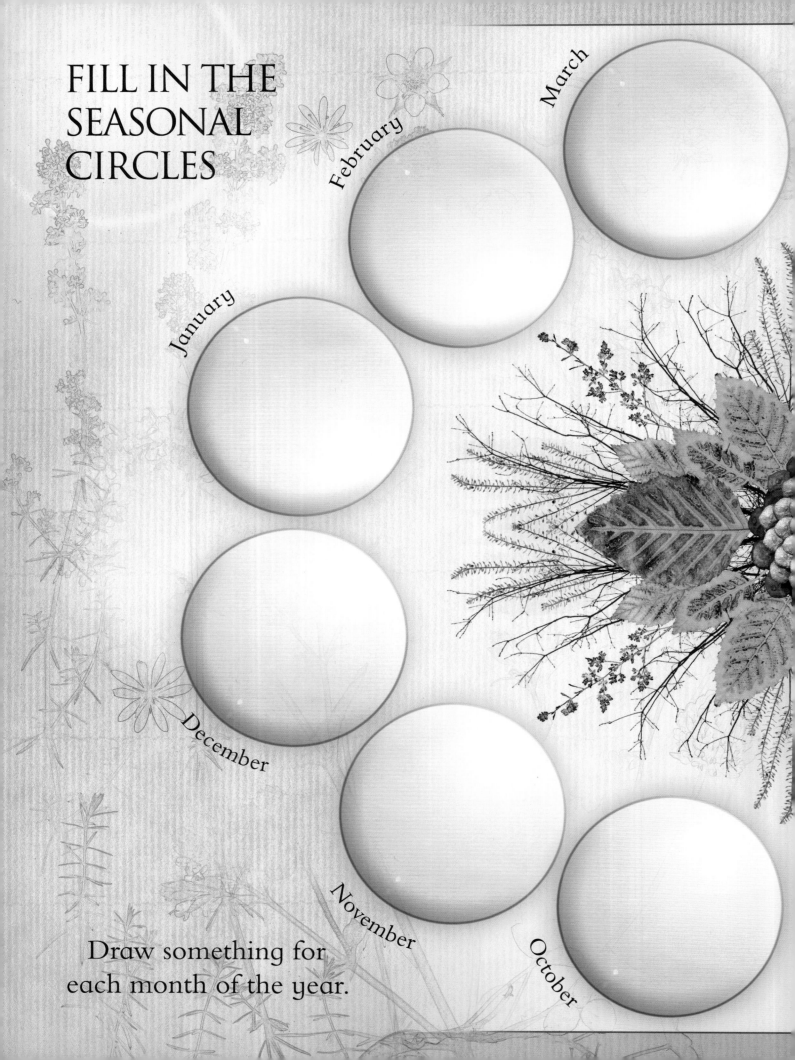

Draw something for each month of the year.

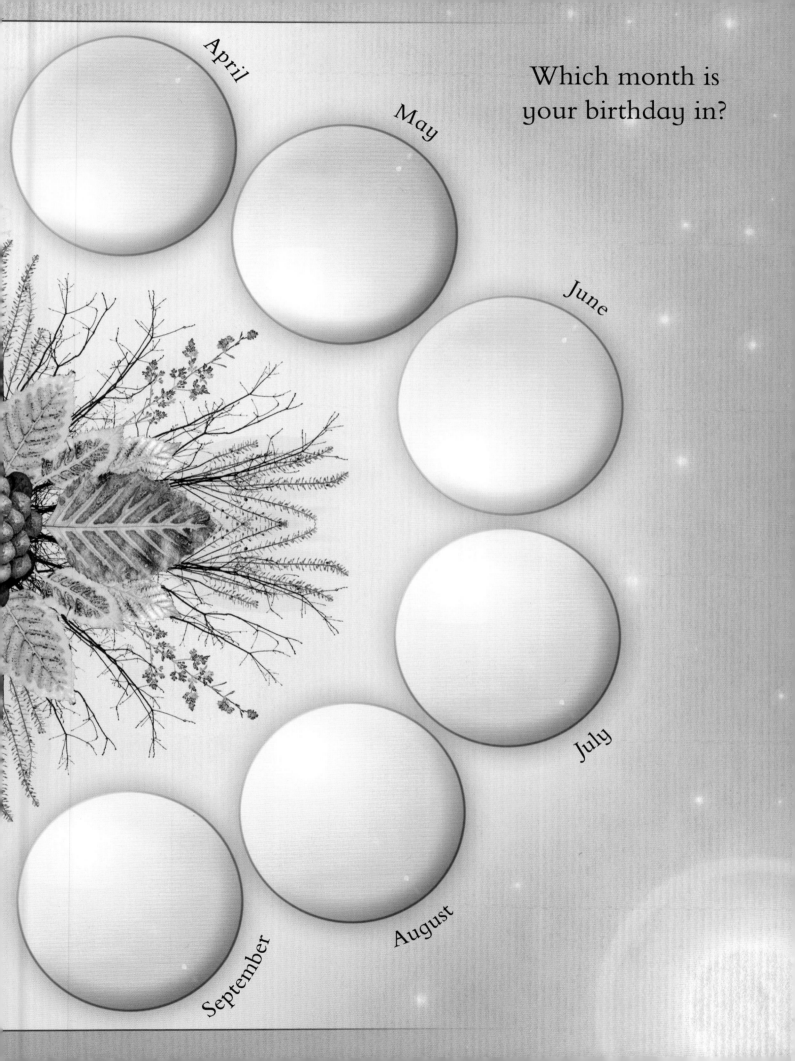

Which month is
your birthday in?

April

May

June

July

August

September

GET OUT ALL YEAR ROUND

catkins

blue tit

bumblebee

bracken

daffodil

dragonfly

frog

brimstone

SPRING

WINTER

yew

wren

snowflakes

feather

lichen

holly

crow

animal tracks

pine cone

dandelion

caterpillar

honey bee

poppy

gatekeeper

goldfinch

grasshopper

ladybird

beetle

lizard

SUMMER

AUTUMN

acorns

banded snail

daddy-long-legs

comma

spider

rose hips

toadstool

winged seeds

conkers

blackberries

Tick all the plants and animals you have seen this year.

DID YOU KNOW?

The ancient Romans used to rub nettles on their
bodies to help them keep warm. Ouch!

Garden snails have lots of
teeth, but you can't see them.

You have two eyelids on each
eye, but owls have three.

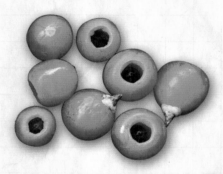

Woodpeckers can
peck up to 20
times a second.

Yew berries and leaves are
poisonous but the leaves
are also used for medicine.

Ash was once used to
make spears because it
is springy and straight.

Pigs can't sweat, so they roll
in mud to stay cool.

Toads change colour to match
the soil in which they live.

Light is made up of seven colours,
which you see when sun shines through raindrops.

A ladybird's
spots fade as
it gets older.

A cow's stomach has four parts:
the rumen, the reticulum, the
omasum and the abomasum.

Only female
bumblebees
can sting.

Buttercups like
damp places.
Their Latin name
means little frog.

Dragonflies spend most of their
lives underwater as nymphs.

Female blue
tits prefer the
males with the
yellowest chests.

Slugs easily dry out so they
prefer damp, cool places.

Every snowflake has six
points. Try counting them.

WHOSE POOS?

Draw a line between each animal
and its droppings.

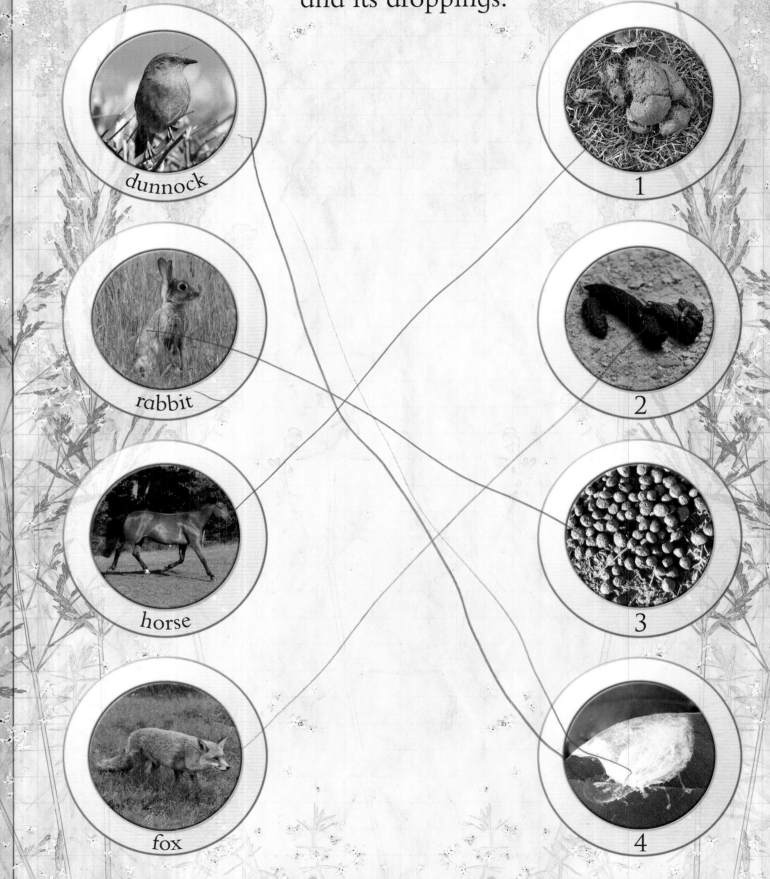

dunnock

rabbit

horse

fox

1

2

3

4

NATURE'S CODE

Fill in the blanks using the words listed below.

When you're outside having _ _ _,
there are some things you must remember,
at every time of year
from New Year's Day until December:
Keep all _ _ _ _ under control,
as they might scare cows or sheep
Stay away from ponds or rivers
as they may be very _ _ _ _.
Leaving _ _ _ _ _ _ on the ground
is a really horrid habit.
What if something plastic
were to choke a passing rabbit?
Don't stray from _ _ _ _ _ _ _ _ signs
as you might soon find you're lost
or in a field marked "_ _ _ _"
or by a farmer who is cross!
Leave the things you find outside
for other people to discover,
for that's what clever _ _ _ _ _ _ _ _ do
who are true nature lovers.

children   *bull*   *footpath*   *dogs*
fun   *deep*   *litter*

DISCOVER THE ANSWERS

HELP THE WORKER BEE

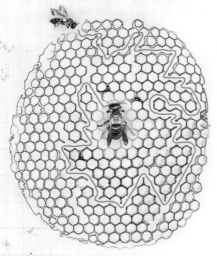

CAN YOU GUESS?
1) flower 2) leaf
3) snail 4) fish
5) bird (pheasant) 6) sweetcorn
7) eggs 8) dragonfly
9) turkey 10) hedgehog
11) seaweed 12) mushroom

WHAT DO I TURN INTO?
1) frog 2) dragonfly
3) ladybird 4) butterfly

FIND THE FAMILIES
DEER: fawn, stag, doe
HENS: chick, cockerel, hen
SHEEP: lamb, ram, ewe
COWS: calf, bull, cow
DUCKS: duckling, drake, duck
GOATS: kid, billy, nanny

ANIMAL GROUPS
MAMMALS: pig, water vole
INVERTEBRATES: stag beetle, spider
BIRDS: great tit, robin
REPTILES: lizard
FISH: barbel
AMPHIBIAN: newt

TICK THE TRUE FACTS
TRUE: 1, 3, 4, 5, 10
FALSE: 2, 6, 7, 8 9

WHO'S HIDING HERE?

WHO'S MY PARTNER?
1) cockerel 2) pheasant
3) peacock 4) sparrow
5) mallard 6) chaffinch

FIND THE MATCHING PAIRS

CAN YOU GUESS?
1) butterfly 2) nettle
3) donkey 4) pine cone
5) blackberries 6) dandelion
7) cow 8) shell
9) frog 10) bumblebee
11) apple 12) feather

SPOT THE DIFFERENCE

NAME THAT GROUP
Butterflies = a flutter
Lizards = a lounge
Cows = a herd
Geese = a gaggle
Turkeys = a gang
Otters = a raft

SPOT THE DIFFERENCE

ODD ONE OUT
Bee • Harebell • Butterfly • Duckling

TICK THE TRUE FACTS
TRUE: 3, 5, 6, 7, 10
FALSE: 1, 2, 4, 8, 9

SOLVE THE RIDDLES
Robin • Holly • Deer • Icicles

WHOSE POOS?
1) horse 2) fox
3) rabbit 4) bird

NATURE'S CODE
Line 1 = FUN
Line 5 = DOGS
Line 8 = DEEP
Line 9 = LITTER
Line 13 = FOOTPATH
Line 15 = BULL
Line 19 = CHILDREN

Title page quotation is
from the poem "in Just–"
by E.E. Cummings